Bats

Returning Wildlife

Bats

John E. Becker

KIDHAVEN PRESS

THOMSON

——————— ✦ ———————™

GALE

Detroit • New York • San Diego • San Francisco
Boston • New Haven, Conn. • Waterville, Maine
London • Munich

*To my daughter, Janean, who has always supported
and encouraged her dad*

Library of Congress Cataloging-in-Publication Data

Becker, John E., 1942–
  Bats / by John E. Becker.
    p. cm. — (Returning wildlife)
  Includes bibliographical references.
    Summary: Discusses bat anatomy, their habits, and habitats;
prejudices against bats; their decline in numbers; their importance
to the environment; and conservation efforts.
    ISBN 0-7377-1009-8 (hard: alk. paper)
    1. Bats—Juvenile literature. [1. Bats. 2. Endangered species.
3. Wildlife conservation.] I. Title. II. Series.
    QL737.C5 B385 2002
    599.4—dc21

                                                    2001003957

Copyright 2002 by KidHaven Press,
an imprint of The Gale Group
10911 Technology Place, San Diego, CA 92127

Printed in the U.S.A.

Contents

chapter 1

Misunderstood

Throughout history, bats have been misunderstood. In Western civilizations, people believe that bats are associated with vampires, witches, and the devil. Bats are also feared as carriers of deadly diseases like **rabies**. Yet in some parts of the world, such as China, bats are considered "good luck."

Bats live in every part of the world except extreme desert and polar regions. They are second only to rodents as the most numerous type of mammal. However, bat populations have declined because of the actions of human beings. Habitat destruction, vandalism, people disturbing bats as they rest in caves, and the use of pesticides have all contributed to the loss of bats.

Bats Around the World

Bats have been on earth for more than 65 million years. Bat skeletons preserved in oil-shale deposits in Germany show that ancient bats looked the same as today's bats. It is also believed that they navigated by using sound waves, like modern bats.

A bat hovers over an angry witch. Some people once thought of bats as evil.

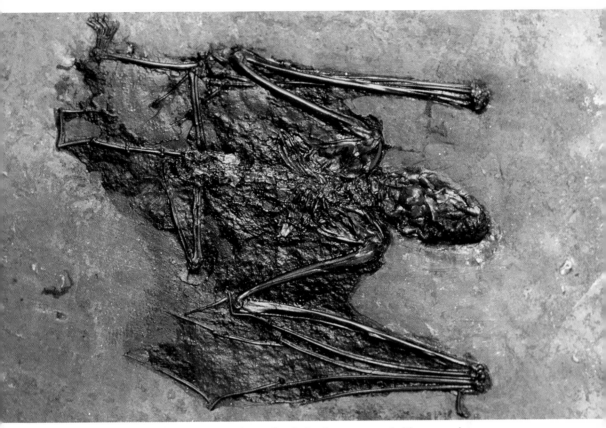

An ancient bat, preserved as a fossil, looks very much like a modern bat.

Bats are grouped together in the mammalian order **Chiroptera**, a word formed from two Greek words meaning "hand-wing." They get this name because their arm and finger bones are extended, giving bats the ability to fly by using their webbed hands.

There are almost one thousand species of bats around the world. Until recently, bats living in the United States that were declining in numbers seemed to have little hope of recovering.

For example, more than half of the forty-five species of bats found in the United States are disappearing, and six of these species are on the U.S. endangered species list.

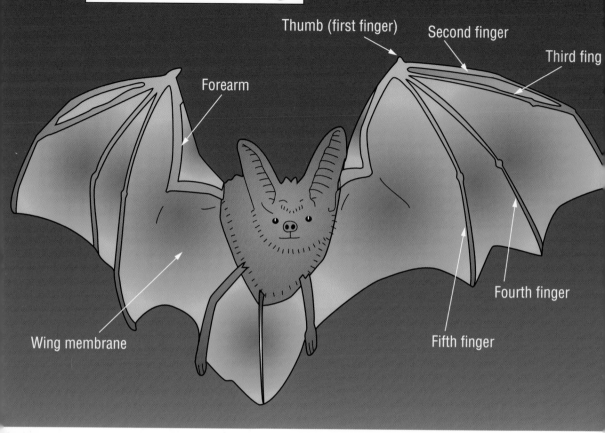

The Bat's "Hand-Wing"

Thumb (first finger)

Second finger

Third fing

Forearm

Wing membrane

Fourth finger

Fifth finger

They include the gray bat, greater long-nosed bat, Hawaiian hoary bat, Indiana bat, lesser long-nosed bat, and two subspecies of the Townsend's big-eared bat, the Ozark big-eared bat and the Virginia big-eared bat.

Some, like the Indiana bat, are continuing to disappear despite people's best efforts to save them. Another twenty species of bats are listed as being of "special concern." Bat conservationists believe that several other species are also in trouble.

The Importance of Bats

Bats play a vitally important role in the balance of nature. As scientists study bats and learn more about them, it has become clear that they are some of nature's most useful animals. One way that bats help humans is by eating insects. A bat may eat its own body weight in insects each night.

Studies of the 20 million Brazilian free-tailed bats in Bracken Cave in Texas showed that they ate over two hundred tons of insects in one night. Across the country, bats eat a staggering number of insects yearly. Their role in nature is not limited to eating insects, however.

A Mexican free-tailed bat captures a tasty moth (top). Free-tailed bats emerging from Bracken Cave will eat millions of insects in one night.

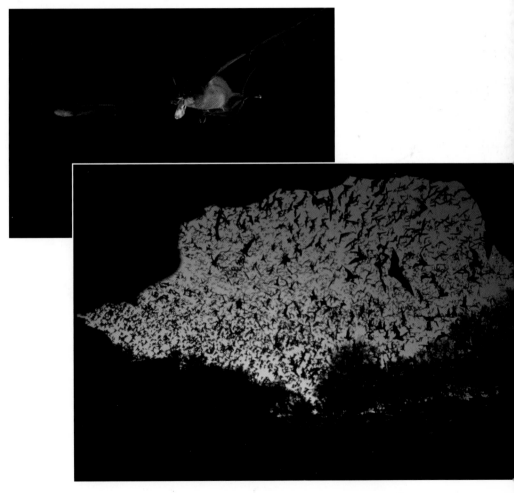

Some bats primarily eat fruit and nectar. These bats are important to the growth of fruit trees. By eating the seeds of the fruits and then releasing the seeds in their droppings, these bats help spread the seeds over a large area. This process, known as seed dispersal, is an important function that bats perform in tropical areas around the world.

By consuming nectar from flowering plants, some bats serve as pollinators. Bats spread pollen from one plant to another in the same way as bees and butterflies. Thus, they play a key role in the reproduction of those plants. A number of flowering plants are almost entirely dependent on bats for **pollination**.

A hungry bat zeros in on the rich fruit of a cactus.

In some areas, bat droppings, known as **guano**, are used extensively as a natural fertilizer. Some caves, with huge deposits of guano, are mined for this valuable material. During the Civil War, the Confederate army mined guano deposits and used them as an ingredient in the manufacture of gunpowder. Carlsbad Caverns in New Mexico yielded thousands of tons of guano in the early 1900s.

Bats are also some of nature's most fascinating animals. By studying bats and learning about their behaviors, scientists hope to solve some of the mysteries surrounding these amazing creatures.

Bat Facts

Bats weigh from a fraction of an ounce to over three pounds. The bumblebee bat of Thailand weighs around two grams (less than a penny). The Samoan flying fox weighs over three pounds and has a wingspan of over six feet. The largest bat in the United States is the greater mastiff bat with a wingspan of twenty-two inches.

Bats are the only mammals in the world that can fly. Some other mammals, such as flying squirrels, may glide, but only bats have mastered true flight. Extended arm and finger bones connected by skin allow bats to "fly with their hands." An **aerodynamic** shape, large wings, and powerful muscles give bats the necessary characteristics for flight. Their ability to twist and turn in the air to capture insects is truly remarkable.

"Blind as a bat" is an expression used to describe someone who does not see very well. Bats actually see quite well. But it is not a bat's eyesight that allows it to hunt insects at night.

"Echolocation" gives a bat the ability to fly swiftly through a dark night, catch prey in flight, and avoid tree

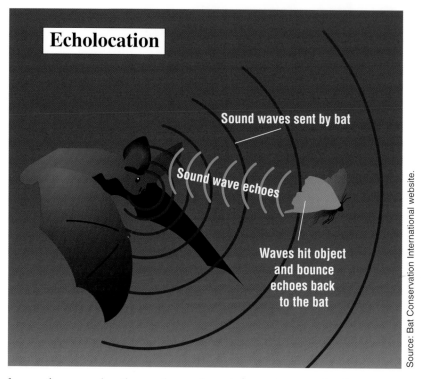

Source: Bat Conservation International website.

branches and other obstacles. A bat uses echolocation the same way a submarine uses **sonar** to locate objects. The flying bat sends out high-frequency sound waves from its mouth. When the sound waves reach an object, they bounce off and echo back to the bat. From the echoes, bats develop an acoustic (sound-based) image of the surrounding environment. Bats can determine size, shape, texture, and how an insect is moving. Bats' ears are so sensitive that they can detect something as thin as a strand of human hair. The bat can also determine how far away it is from an object. In a matter of seconds, a bat can identify an insect, catch it, and eat it—all in total darkness. It could be said that bats "see with their ears."

Most bats in the United States feed exclusively on insects. Other bats in North America and around the world eat a wide variety of foods. Bats eat fruit, nectar, pollen, birds, fish, lizards, frogs, and mice. False vampire bats even eat other bats.

True vampire bats drink the blood of other animals such as cows, pigs, goats, and chickens. Only rarely do they attack humans. Despite that fact, many bats have been killed because of the fear of vampire bats. Vampire bats are found in Mexico, Central America, and South America.

Any place where insects are found in the United States can be considered bat habitat. Forested areas, the air above lakes and streams, farms, and cities are considered prime bat habitats because of the large numbers of insects found in those places. Unfortunately,

After biting a chicken's foot, a vampire bat slurps up the blood.

some bats, such as the endangered Indiana bat, are dwindling in numbers because of loss of their habitat. The forest areas along streams, which Indiana bats prefer for hunting insects, are disappearing. A suitable bat habitat must also include places for the bats to rest.

Where a bat rests when it is not flying is called a **roost**. Bats roost in places that are free of predators, have suitable temperatures for bats, allow the bats to eat, sleep, mate, raise their young, and hibernate in the winter. Bat roosting sites include hollow trees, tree bark, leaves, buildings, caves, mines, and bridges.

Some of the most important roosting sites for bats are abandoned mines. In the past, when mines were abandoned, they were oftentimes sealed to prevent people from exploring the potentially dangerous sites. Over the past several years, many of those mine en-

Bats roost on the beam of a barn where they are warm and safe.

trances have been fitted with gates that keep people out, but allow bats to come and go freely. One abandoned mine in Wisconsin currently is home to a **colony** of at least one hundred thousand bats.

When there are no insects to eat during the winter, some bats, such as gray bats, find roosting sites where they can hibernate. During **hibernation** bats reduce their body temperature to just above freezing to match the surrounding cave temperature. They also slow their breathing and other body functions to the lowest possible level. Throughout the winter the bats will hang from the roof of the cave in a deep sleep. Bats may hibernate for as long as seven months.

Critical Times for Bats

If people enter caves while bats are hibernating, the bats will awaken, raise their body temperature, and take flight. Such activity takes precious energy reserves that the bats have stored for the winter. If the bats are disturbed too often, they will use up their energy reserves before insects are available to eat in the spring. Many bats could starve to death under those circumstances. Even people with no intention of harming bats could cause great harm by exploring a cave while bats are hibernating.

Other bats, such as red bats, deal with the shortage of insects by flying south for the winter. Several species of tree bats **migrate** over long distances, like birds. Some bats migrate from Canada to the southern United States or Mexico, traveling as far as eight hundred miles. These bats remain active all winter hunting for insects as they do during the summer months. Scientists believe that migrating bats follow the same route between their summer and winter hunting grounds each year.

How the bats are able to find their way back to their homes, known as **homing instinct**, is a mystery to scientists. In one experiment, fifteen hundred bats were removed from a cave in Kentucky and transported two hundred miles away. The bats were banded (had a tag or band attached in order to identify them later) and released. Most of the bats managed to find their way back home.

Another critical time for cave dwelling bats is summer, when females roost together in **maternity colonies**. Pregnant females gather together by the hundreds or even thousands to begin roosting in early spring. They choose caves with warm air temperatures, and, by clustering together, temperatures become even warmer. The warmer a roost, the faster the pregnancy will proceed. Gestation (the period of time from the beginning of pregnancy to birth) is approximately two months.

Once the **pups** (baby bats) are born, they are totally dependent on their mothers for the first few weeks of their lives. Human disturbances during this

Some bat species fly south for the winter. Others, like those pictured, prefer to hibernate.

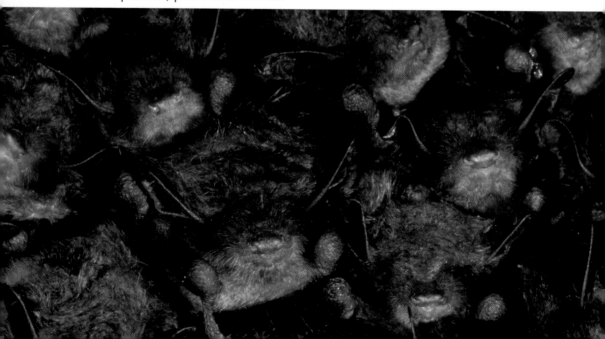

A mother bat cradles her pup.

critical period can be dangerous for young bats. Mother bats, when frightened, may drop their pups or abandon the roost. A high percentage of young may be lost at such times.

Most people are only beginning to understand the value of bats. Unfortunately, bats have suffered from being misunderstood for such an extended time that many species are now disappearing at an alarming rate.

chapter 2

Why Are Bats Disappearing?

For most of the twentieth century, bats steadily declined in numbers across the United States. Their disappearance was related to the fact that bats are more likely to suffer large population losses than other animals. One of the major factors in bats' decline has been their habit of roosting together in large groups. Unlike other small mammals, some bats live together in colonies that may number in the millions. This behavior has resulted in thousands of bats dying from natural disasters such as flooding, or from human disturbances. When such losses occur, bats' low reproductive rate (usually one offspring per year) makes it difficult for the bat population to recover.

Another factor in the disappearance of bats is their need to sleep during the day. Because bats sleep in caves and buildings where they can be easily found, they are at greater risk of attack than other animals. Sleeping bats are easy prey for animal predators or people intent on harming them.

Because bats are easily frightened, they will take flight in panic when disturbed. Under such circumstances many bats could be injured or killed.

People's fear of bats, based on the belief that bats infect humans with deadly diseases, such as rabies, led people to kill bats. Many communities, believing they are ridding themselves of dangerous animals, organize campaigns to destroy any bats found nearby.

Because bats live together in huge groups, many may die at once from natural disasters and from human interference.

Animals such as snakes, owls, hawks, skunks, and raccoons occasionally eat bats. But man bears the responsibility for bats disappearing at a rate that threatens them with extinction. Vandalism of bat roosting sites, and killing bats for sport, was considered acceptable for much of the twentieth century. But even when

19

Beetles lunch on a dead bat here, but people are a far greater threat to bats than animal predators.

people have no intention of harming bats, they can do great harm. People exploring a cave during bat hibernation periods, or when female bats have their young, has resulted in death for many bats. Educating the public about the importance of not disturbing bats at those times is a key element in bat survival.

Rabies

A person bitten by a rabid bat may be infected with rabies. Many bats have been killed because of that fear. In truth, however, bats have infected very few people with rabies. It is relatively uncommon for bats in the United States to have rabies. Even when bats are rabid, they are seldom aggressive toward humans. Fewer than forty people have been infected with rabies from bats in the past fifty years. Many more people die from bee stings, dog attacks, or lightning strikes each year than from contracting rabies from bats.

Animal Predators

In nature's complex system, bats are both predator and prey. Because bats are active mainly after dark, they often fall victim to owls. Owls, like the screech owl, prey on bats as they fly during the night. When bats venture out early in the evening they risk being taken by a hawk or falcon.

Snakes frequently eat bats. In some instances snakes will crawl on the wall of a cave and attack bats as they roost. More often, however, snakes hang from cave openings or nearby trees when bats fly by. If a bat

A bat chirps helplessly as a snake devours it.

makes the slightest contact with a snake, the snake will strike swiftly. A snake may capture up to six bats in an evening. Bats roosting in trees are more susceptible to attacks by snakes than cave dwelling bats.

Before they learn to fly (generally two to five weeks after birth), young bats are relatively defenseless. If one falls to the floor of a cave during that time, a number of predators await it there. Ants, spiders, cockroaches, and centipedes will gladly feed on the helpless bat. Some large spiders attack bats as they roost, or when they are caught in their webs.

Many species of mammals feed on bats from time to time. Opossums, skunks, weasels, raccoons, foxes, bobcats, and domestic dogs and cats will all capture a bat if they can.

Despite the fact that other animals eat bats, they are not a regular part of the diet of any animal. Bat populations are not declining because of animal predators.

Human Threats

The major threat to bat populations across the United States, and around the world, is man. Because of fears and misunderstandings, many people believe that the best way to deal with bats is to kill them. People have shot, poisoned, and set fires to destroy bats. In some cases, people have sealed the entrances to mines to drive bats away. Some communities have hired pest control companies to eliminate bats. Just as often, however, bats have been killed accidentally.

Habitat destruction is one of the primary reasons that bats are disappearing. When people cut down trees, roosting sites for bats are destroyed. Even when old, hollow trees are removed, some bats lose their homes. Cutting down trees at the entrance to a cave

We Can Help Bats

Do not disturb maternity colonies and hibernating bats.

If you must enter caves, leave everything as you found it.

Never harm bats. Bats are extremely beneficial.

Source: Michael J. Harvey, et al, *Bats of the United States,* published by the Arkansas Game and Fish Commission.

may change the temperature in the cave. Even slight changes in temperature may make it impossible for bats to live in a cave. Hibernating bats need temperatures slightly above freezing, and removing trees may cause the cave temperature to drop below freezing. When caves are used for tours and other human activities, bats are driven from their roosts. As human populations continue to grow, more and more bat habitat is destroyed.

Vandalism, such as throwing objects at bats, making loud noises, or setting fires in caves, has taken a heavy toll on bats. If vandals enter a cave and make a disturbance, the resulting panic among the bats may result in many bats dying. What might seem like harmless fun could actually be quite devastating to the local bat population.

When people spray pesticides to eliminate insects, they also eliminate bats that eat insects. Pesticide poisoning has been identified as a contributing factor in the decline of Mexican free-tailed bats in the United

Merlin Tuttle, founder of Bat Conservation International, inspects bats killed by pesticides.

States. Pesticides sprayed on fruits continue to pose a threat to fruit-eating bats. People wash fruits to remove pesticides, but bats eat fruit that may be coated with pesticides.

Hope for a Comeback

Efforts to save bats have been slow to develop. But now that more people are aware of the plight of bats, programs have been set in place to bring them back. Those programs have given conservation-minded people hope that most species of bats can be saved.

Bat Conservation

The U.S. government, state wildlife departments, private conservation organizations, and many individuals across the country are now actively involved in bat conservation. The first step in the conservation process is to educate people about the role bats play in the environment. Educational programs, designed to correct people's misconceptions about bats, are beginning to produce positive results.

Conservation projects, such as constructing gates at the entrance to caves to prevent people from entering caves during hibernation and maternity seasons, are also helping bats recover.

Organizations Helping Bats

The number of organizations, both governmental and private, committed to helping bats is growing each year. Without the involvement of these organizations and private individuals, bat populations would stand little chance of recovering.

The U.S. Fish and Wildlife Service has played a major role in restoring bat populations. Among a number of noteworthy contributions, that agency has produced educational information about bats and purchased important caves so bats could be protected. Other federal agencies involved in bat conservation include the U.S. Forest Service, National Park Service, Bureau of Land Management, and Soil Conservation Service. The Tennessee Valley Authority has assisted in efforts to save

Scientists fit bats with transmitters to follow their movements.

bats in the southeastern part of the country. And many state wildlife agencies have established programs to protect the bats found within their borders.

A number of private organizations have also made important contributions to saving bats. Some of the leading organizations are Bat Conservation International, Cave Research Foundation, American Cave Conservation Association, and Nature Conservancy.

The National Speleological Society (NSS), a national organization for **cavers** (cave explorers), has educated its members and others about the danger of harming bats when people explore caves during hibernation or maternity seasons. NSS now plays an important role in the conservation of bats and other forms of life found in caves.

Gray Bats

Gray bats (scientific name *Myotis grisescens*) are found primarily in caves in Alabama, Arkansas, Kentucky, Missouri, and Tennessee. They are medium-sized, gray-colored, and weigh three-tenths to four-tenths of an ounce. The wingspan of a gray bat is eleven to thirteen inches. Gray bats live in caves year-round, but use different caves in summer and winter. They hibernate in

Young gray bats pack themselves into a dense cluster.

cold caves in the winter. During the summer, female gray bats cluster together in large, warm caves in maternity colonies that may consist of a few hundred to many thousands of bats.

Because almost all of the gray bats found in the United States hibernate in just eight caves, many thousands could die in a single disaster. In 1969, gray bats were disappearing so rapidly that scientists predicted they would soon become extinct. Prior to that, it was estimated that gray bat hibernation caves each supported between 100,000 and 1.5 million bats. When hibernating colonies were recounted in 1979, most contained only 10,000 to 50,000 bats.

By 1982 it was estimated that fewer than 1.6 million gray bats survived in the United States. In that year the Gray Bat Recovery Plan was developed. Building gates or fences was a critical part of the plan.

Protecting Gray Bats

In 1985 several organizations joined forces to protect an extremely important cave for gray bats in Tennessee. Hubbards Cave, ranked as one of the three most important hibernating sites for bats in America, needed to be protected from humans. The Tennessee National Guard, Tennessee Nature Conservancy, National Speleological Society, Mid-State Steel Corporation, U.S. Fish and Wildlife Service, and Cave Conservation Institute worked together to construct the largest gate for bats ever built at the time. The massive structure measured 30 feet tall by 35 feet wide and consisted of 130 tons of concrete and steel.

By 1986, gray bats had dramatically increased their numbers due to reduced disturbance of their cave roosts. Three of the most important gray bat caves in

Tennessee and Alabama had increased their populations by 80 percent.

In Missouri, gray bats have occupied more than 125 caves. Four caves are used for hibernation. Two of those caves are fenced to keep humans out while the bats are hibernating. From the late 1970s to the present, gray bat populations in these caves have increased by over 75 percent. Of the approximately thirty-six maternity caves in Missouri, nine are fenced or gated. Populations in these maternity caves have increased nearly 40 percent during the past twenty-five years.

Workmen tackle the huge job of gating Hubbards Cave in 1985.

Gray bats have now recovered so well across their range that the Gray Bat Recovery Team will soon recommend that they be reduced from "endangered" to "threatened" status. This represents a significant milestone in the conservation of bats in the United States.

Virginia Big-Eared Bats

Virginia big-eared bats (*Corynorhinus townsendii virginianus*) live in caves in Kentucky, North Carolina, Virginia, and West Virginia. They are medium-sized bats weighing less than half an ounce. Virginia big-eared bats are easily recognized by their large ears (more than one

A scientist carefully displays a Virginia big-eared bat. Only scientists should handle bats.

inch long) and sizable bumps (glands) on either side of the nose. They are a light to dark brown color, with a twelve- to thirteen-inch wingspan. Virginia big-eared bats hibernate in groups consisting of just a few individuals to over five thousand.

Virginia big-eared bats, like other cave dwelling bats, are vulnerable to disturbances of their roosting sites in caves. Vandalism and other forms of human disturbances led to the decline of Virginia big-eared bats during the twentieth century. By 1979 their numbers had dropped so low that they were listed as endangered.

Only eighty-five hundred Virginia big-eared bats were thought to survive by 1984. The Virginia Big-Eared Bat Recovery Plan recommended that signs be placed at cave entrances, and that gates or fences be built there to prevent disturbances.

After a gate was constructed at the entrance to a cave in North Carolina in 1986, the Virginia big-eared bat colony in that cave doubled in size each year over the next three years. By 1988 the bat population there had increased from 17 to 139 bats. At that time, only 10,000 Virginia big-eared bats were known to exist.

Increasing Numbers

West Virginia has the largest population of Virginia big-eared bats. Wildlife officials in that state have studied bat movements with radio-tracking devices, joined with other governmental agencies and private organizations to protect caves, and educated the public about the importance of bats. Approximately ten thousand Virginia big-eared bats now live in West Virginia.

In the four states where they are found in the eastern United States, Virginia big-eared bats have increased

A group of Virginia big-eared bats hibernate in a cave. Their numbers have increased a lot since 1984.

significantly in numbers. Today, there are over eighteen thousand—more than double the 1984 population.

Gray bats and Virginia big-eared bats are excellent examples of how people have helped bats recover. Unfortunately, many species of bats in the United States continue to diminish in numbers. The first few decades of the twenty-first century, therefore, will be critical for bats as they struggle for survival.

Can Bats Survive?

A rapid clicking sound coming from a high-frequency receiver told the waiting wildlife officers that the bats were beginning to leave their cave. It was a beautiful June night in the mountains of West Virginia. The air was filled with the bats' favorite food—moths. Suddenly the clicking sounds increased as one bat after another flew through the small cave entrance.

The sight of so many Virginia big-eared bats soaring into the evening sky brought a smile to the faces of those waiting outside the cave. West Virginia Wildlife Resources biologists were here to count the bats, as they do each year. Using night vision scopes that see clearly into the darkened cave, they are able to get an accurate count of the bats. Each year the number has gone up. When the count began in 1983, this cave had 160 bats. In 2001, 900 bats were counted.

Efforts such as these, and the building of gates and fences to keep people out of bat caves at hibernation and maternity seasons,

This night vision scope helps scientists observe bats in the dark.

have allowed the Virginia big-eared bat population to soar in West Virginia.

"We work very hard to keep accurate population figures each year," explained wildlife biologist Craig Stihler. "We have also studied Virginia big-eared bats to determine the habitats they feed in, and how far they travel from their caves. What we have learned about their behavior has helped us to bring them back."

West Virginia's success at increasing the numbers of Virginia big-eared bats is an example that other states hope to follow with their bats.

Scientists use radio-tracking devices to learn about the travel and feeding habits of bats.

Bats Still Declining in Numbers

Unfortunately, despite efforts to save them, many species of bats in the United States are continuing to decline in numbers. While gray bats might soon be taken off the endangered species list, several other species could be added in the near future. Cave dwelling bats seem to be especially at risk, and are still disappearing at a rapid rate.

The decline of the Indiana bat (*Myotis sodalis*), despite conservation efforts on its behalf, has scientists searching for answers. Found throughout much of the eastern United States, these small bats (weighing two-tenths to three-tenths of an an ounce) hibernate in caves during the winter. Currently fewer than 400,000 of these bats survive. Indiana bats have been found in over 300 caves in 20 states. One-half of all Indiana bats hibernate in only 8 caves in 3 states, however.

The situation for Indiana bats in Kentucky and Missouri is particularly distressing to scientists. From 1960 to 1975, approximately 647,000 Indiana bats were hibernating in these states. By 2001 the numbers of Indiana bats in Kentucky and Missouri had dropped to 121,000—a decline of over 80 percent. Such a rapid loss is of great concern because the conservation measures for Indiana bats have not halted the population losses.

The picture is not entirely bleak, however. Indiana bat populations in the northern part of their geographic range have increased by 25 percent since 1975. Scientists are trying to determine the cause for these differences. If the reasons for the decline can be identified and controlled, Indiana bats may, one day, return to safe population levels throughout their range.

An Indiana bat. Populations of Indiana bats are still declining in some states.

People Helping Bats

As people learn more about bats, greater numbers are working to help them survive. From gating abandoned mines to building bat houses, people are finding ways to get involved in bat conservation.

One way that people help bats is by building bat houses. The houses, similar to birdhouses, are constructed to attract bats and thereafter provide a permanent roosting site. One successful bat house is located on the campus of the University of Florida in Gainesville, Florida. The house shelters a colony of eighty thousand Brazilian free-tailed bats. This is the largest colony of bats living in a home built specifically for bats anywhere in the United States.

Kids are also helping bats. In Cincinnati, Ohio, they assisted in a study of Eastern Pipistrelle bats that revealed new information about that species' behavior. Kids from the Cincinnati Nature Center helped by observing bats for this important study. Children in Riverside, California, competed in an art contest that helped focus attention on the importance of bats. And throughout Mexico, the young are learning about bats and helping to protect their roosting sites through the Program for the Conservation of Migratory Bats.

Bats return to their bat house after a night of hunting.

Bat Conservation International

One organization, solely focused on the conservation of bats, is Bat Conservation International (BCI). In 1982, Merlin D. Tuttle, a field biologist who had been studying bats since 1959, founded BCI. For several years Tuttle had been increasingly concerned about the rapid decline in bat populations around the world. It was obvious to him that bats would continue to disappear until people were educated about the importance of bats.

Bat expert Merlin Tuttle offers a banana to a hungry bat.

The bumblebee bat, which weighs less than a penny, is now protected in Thailand.

Providing educational materials about bats, therefore, has been one of the primary functions of BCI. In its first year of existence BCI distributed a pamphlet entitled *Bats and Public Health* to state health departments across the country. That pamphlet helped eliminate many misunderstandings about bats and the "threat" they pose to humans. Each year since that time BCI has produced and distributed educational materials that have significantly increased people's understanding of bats.

In its second year, BCI helped secure permanent protection for Judges Cave in Florida. That cave houses one of the most important bat nursery colonies in eastern North America. Working with local organizations, BCI has helped provide protective gates at more than a thousand cave entrances across the country.

BCI works with local groups to encourage the use of bridges as roosting sites for bats. The Bats and Bridges project has become one of BCI's most successful programs.

People stare in awe at a sky darkened by vast numbers of bats.

BCI has also promoted bat conservation in many other countries around the world. Countries, such as Thailand, have provided protection for their bats because of encouragement received from BCI.

Reason for Hope

The future for bats in the United States is by no means secure. Much work remains to be done before these vitally important animals can be considered safe from extinction. Yet with the understanding and assistance of people across the country, bats may once again fill the night skies.

aerodynamic: A streamlined shape.

cavers: People who explore caves.

Chiroptera: The mammalian order in which bats are placed.

colonies: Groups of animals that live together.

echolocation: The sending out of sounds that bounce off objects and echo back, allowing the sender to locate the source of the echo.

guano: Accumulated bat droppings.

hibernation: A state in which bodily functions such as breathing and heart rate slow down in cold temperatures, leading to inactivity.

homing instinct: A learned ability used by animals to find their way home over long distances.

maternity colony: A group of female bats that live and raise their young together.

migration: To travel from one place to another and back again, usually at times of seasonal changes.

pollination: A process in which a pollinator, such as a bat or bee, fertilizes flowers by carrying pollen from one plant to another.

pup: A baby bat.

rabies: A deadly viral disease found only in mammals, transmitted by the bite of an infected animal.

roost: A resting place.

sonar: The use of sound to detect an object.

Books and Periodicals

Diane Ackerman, *Bats: Shadows in the Night.* New York: Crown Publishers, 1997. Author's story of traveling across Texas in search of bats with Merlin Tuttle.

Phyllis J. Perry, *Bats: The Amazing Upside-Downers.* New York: Franklin Watts, 1998. Examines the variations in bats, including their behaviors, physiology, and conservation requirements.

Laurence Pringle, *Batman: Exploring the World of Bats.* New York: Charles Scribner's Sons, 1991. Story of Merlin Tuttle, founder of Bat Conservation International, and his efforts on behalf of the world's bats.

Dee Stuart, *Bats: Mysterious Flyers of the Night.* Minneapolis: Carolrhoda Books, 1994. Looks at the migration, feeding, and other behaviors of bats. Excellent color photographs throughout.

Kathy Wollard, "Seeing Bats in a New Light," *Newsday,* May 11, 1999. Covers basic bat facts such as echolocation, vision, and food preferences.

Organization to Contact

Bat Conservation International
PO Box 162603
Austin, TX 78716
(512) 327-9721
website: www.batcon.org

This organization provides educational information about bats and helps protect bats and their habitats.

Websites

Bats
http://edu.leeds.ac.uk/~edu/technology/epb97/forest/bats.htm

This site provides information about forest bats in England, much of which is applicable to U.S. forest bats as well.

Bats4Kids

http://members.aol.com/bats4kids

This site provides educational information about bats for kids.

Videos

The Bat House Builder's Video. Austin, TX: Bat Conservation International, 2000. An introduction to bat house builders and the successful houses they have used to attract bats to yards, parks, and farms.

The Secret World of Bats. Austin, TX. Bat Conservation International. An award-winning video that covers various aspects of bat behavior around the world.

Acknowledgments

Jacqueline J. Belwood, Ph.D., Cincinnati Nature Center

Susan Boggs, Columbus and Franklin County Metropolitan Park District

Rick Clawson, Missouri Department of Conservation

Robert Currie, U.S. Fish and Wildlife Service

Barbara French, Bat Conservation International

Michael J. Harvey, Tennessee Technological University

Richard Mills, World Discovery Safaris

Craig Stihler, West Virginia Division of Natural Resources

Dr. John E. Becker writes children's books and magazine articles about nature and wild animals. He graduated from Ohio State University in the field of education. He has been an elementary school teacher, college professor, zoo administrator, and has worked in the field of wildlife conservation with the International Society for Endangered Cats. He currently lives in Delaware, Ohio, and teaches writing at the Thurber Writing Academy. He also enjoys visiting schools and sharing his love of writing with kids. In his spare time, Dr. Becker likes to read, hike in the woods, ice skate, and play tennis.

DN   8/03